Australian
ANIMAL VERSES

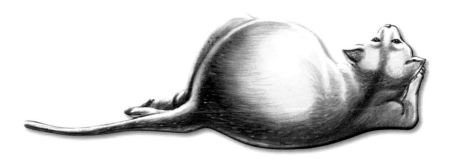

Written by Colin Thiele
Illustrated by Wendy DePaauw

Published by Hinkler Books Pty Ltd
45–55 Fairchild Street
Heatherton Victoria 3202 Australia
www.hinklerbooks.com

First published by Weldon Kids Pty Ltd 1994

© Illustration and design Weldon Kids Pty Ltd
© Text Colin Thiele
© Cover design Hinkler Books Pty Ltd 2010

Editor: Avril Janks
Calligrapher: Meg Dunworth
Cover design: Ruth Comey
Prepress: Graphic Print Group

ISBN: 978 1 7418 5289 9

Printed and bound in China

Australian
ANIMAL VERSES

Written by Colin Thiele
Illustrated by Wendy DePaauw

Sulphur Crest, Sulphur Crest
Screeches in the morning,
The colours in his topknot spread
Like new day dawning.

Sugar glider, airy rider,

How do you travel so?

With limbs spread wide I slide and glide

Where welcoming paperbarks grow.

fairy penguin went to sea
With a fishy notion,
Used his flippers as his wings
And soared beneath the ocean.

*D*ugong, dugong, roaming and free,

Grazing on grasses beneath the sea,

Mermaid or not, you never stay,

But dive below and slip away.

Kookaburra sits on a kurrajong tree,
Kookaburra laughs and laughs at me;
How can it be when day's begun
That he finds the morning so much fun?

Lyre bird, lyre bird, shy and fey
Dance with your magical tail's display,
What is the sound you will mimic today —
A parrot or plover or farmer's dray?

Kangaroo with leaps and jumps
Goes bounding over fallen stumps,
But joey in her pouch inside
Must have a bump-bump-bumpy ride.

Quokka bounced across the clearing
With a quick and nimble hop,
Till a small sound in the bushes
Brought him to a wary stop.

*R*ingtail Possum, stealing blossom,

When I catch you by surprise

You suspect me and inspect me

With your big and bulbous eyes.

Bandicoot,

Now here, now there,

Pokes his snoot

In everywhere.

Platypus was made to be
The strangest creature ever,
Digging in the muddy bank
Beside the brimming river;
Webbed feet, duck's bill,
Eggs in a burrow,
Furry coat, fresh milk
For babies tomorrow . . .
No wonder people make a fuss
Each time they see a platypus.

Where warrigal the dingo
Roams by night
The hills lie lonely
And the stars shine bright;
Points his nose
At the high wide sky
And fills the stillness
With his sad sad cry.

Tasmanian Devils have a threatening stance
And peer at people with a surly glance,
But though they're branded renegades and pests
They're not as nasty as their name suggests.

GLOSSARY

SULPHUR-CRESTED COCKATOOS

These birds from the parrot family have a clever warning system. While the flock scratches about on the ground for seed, grain, roots and nuts, lookouts are on guard in the trees. When danger approaches, they raise their crests and screech as a warning to the flock so they can fly to safety.

SUGAR GLIDERS

These little possums are so quick, as they glide from tree branch to tree branch, that they can catch insects in flight. They can turn themselves into possum parachutes, and glide for about 50 metres at a time. Their tails help them steer while they are flying.

FAIRY PENGUINS

These little creatures are also called Little Penguins, because they are the smallest of all the penguins. They are special birds - the only penguins to breed in Australia, and the only penguins that wait until it's dark before they come in from the sea each day to roost on the land.

DUGONGS

Dugongs aren't fish, but mammals like us, and they breathe air, coming to the surface of the sea to do so. Each dugong can eat an enormous amount of sea grass - as much as 40 kilograms in a day!

KOOKABURRAS

These noisy birds have many other names, like 'Laughing Jack', 'Ha Ha Pigeon', and 'Laughing Kingfisher'. Their call sounds like laughter, and is used to proclaim their territory. They live in families, and the older brothers and sisters help bring up the young birds.

LYREBIRDS

Male lyrebirds put on a show to impress their lady friends. They scratch up some piles of earth to make little platforms for themselves. Then they stand on these platforms, spread their beautiful tails and dance and sing.

KANGAROOS

When baby kangaroos are born, they are blind, and only the size of a bean. They crawl into their mother's pouch, and, depending on what kind of kangaroo they are, stay there for 90 to 270 days. Only the tree kangaroos can move their hind legs separately, when they are walking along branches.

QUOKKAS

These are tree-climbing wallabies, about the size of a cat. When Dutch sailors first saw quokkas on an island off Western Australia in 1658, they thought they were rats ('rott' in Dutch). So they called the island Rottnest Island - and this island still has the name today.

RINGTAIL POSSUMS

These possums use their strong tails as an extra hand, to carry nest materials and also to help them balance while they scramble through trees looking for food. Underneath the tip of the tail, there is a pad of rough skin to give it a better grip.

BANDICOOTS

These little mammals live on the ground, and use their sense of smell to find food. They squeak and grunt as they search for worms and insects.

PLATYPUSES

The strange-looking Platypuses swim with their front feet, one at a time, doing doggy paddle. They use their hind feet for steering, and for brakes. As they swim they hunt for food in the water, using their sensitive beaks to pick up the movements of the small freshwater creatures they like to eat.

DINGOES

Dingoes remind us a lot of dogs, though, unlike dogs, they can't bark. But they have a powerful howl, which can be heard as they move around the outback, looking for dead animals to feast on.

TASMANIAN DEVILS

Tasmanian Devils scream 'Keep away!' at each other when they find the food they like best - dead animals. But these fierce-looking animals can't run very fast, and even rats can outrun and outfight them.

HB

HINKLER
BOOKS